MORE THAN HYMNS 1

HYMN-ANTHEMS FOR
MIXED VOICE CHOIRS

SELECTED AND EDITED BY BARRY ROSE

NOVELLO

LONDON

FRONT COVER photograph of Wells Cathedral Girl Choristers and
Lay Vicars by Tony Bolton
BACK COVER photograph of Barry Rose by Timothy Hands

COVER DESIGN Miranda Harvey

MUSIC SETTING Barnes Music Engraving

NOV 040043
ISBN 0-7119-8880-3

Blessed are the pure in heart, Brightest and best, Fight the good fight,
A Hymn for St. Cecilia, Jesus is the brightest light, Let all mortal
flesh, Let all the world, O perfect love, There is a green hill and When
I needed a neighbour feature on the Lammas Records CD *More than
Hymns* (LAMM 149D) performed by the Choir of Wells Cathedral,
directed by Malcolm Archer, with Rupert Gough, organ

Contents

Preface

Hymns have long been the most enduring musical element in Christian worship, and choirs have good reason to be grateful for a wealth of metrical texts, ranging from the early Latin hymns to those in the more modern idiomatic English of the present day.

In most services, hymns are sung congregationally, but throughout the centuries, composers have been drawn to set new music to texts they have played or sung so often, or to arrange and extend well-loved tunes for use as choir anthems.

This, then, is the basis on which we now welcome you to *More Than Hymns* – a two-volume collection which will bring new and existing anthem-style arrangements to your choir library, together with the original music of composers who have drawn their inspiration from the poetry of hymnody.

With texts of prayer and praise, hope and consolation, coupled with memorable melodies, we hope that there is something here for all choirs who lead worship.

I am grateful to my fellow choral advisers at Novello for their help and advice and to Elizabeth Robinson for her painstaking preparation of these two volumes.

Barry Rose
Somerset, November 2001

Notes on the music

Blessed are the pure in heart · Henry Walford Davies (1869-1941)
Here is a well known text that is actually the first and last verses of a seventeen-verse poem by John Keble (1792-1866) written for the Feast of the Purification of the Virgin Mary (Candlemas). We have retained the original 'cradle' (bar 15) though for more general use, it is possible to sing 'dwelling' at this point, as found in many hymnals. The music, by Henry Walford Davies, is simple and yet highly expressive, and somehow the key of E major seems to suit every voice part. Some other versions give the first two bars as an organ introduction. We have reproduced the version which the composer included in the 1933 *Church Anthem Book*, of which he was co-editor, though he does designate it as 'Duet' at this point – probably for two solo sopranos/trebles. He also marks the first verse to be sung by a quartet, the accompaniment throughout as *ad lib.*

Brightest and best · Eric Thiman (1900-75)
Prior to becoming Bishop of Calcutta, Reginald Heber (1783-1826) was Rector of Hodnet, Shropshire, and it was there that he wrote his well known hymns, including *Brightest and Best*. It was first published a year after his death and since then has been associated with several tunes for congregational use. This setting is taken from Eric Thiman's extended cantata, *The Nativity*, first published by Novello in 1934 whilst the composer was organist at the Congregational Park Chapel, Crouch End, London.

Its lilting melody is immediately memorable, and is an ideal companion to the text. Each performer needs to feel a certain lightness on the third beat of each bar, otherwise some of the less important syllables will end up being stressed. At the half-way point in each verse, your choir will find it necessary to shorten the 3-beat note, in order to take another breath and keep the melody flowing. In the hope of achieving a better choral balance, we have transposed the alto part up an octave in bars 37 to 39 (1st beat) and bars 68 to 70 (1st beat) – though some choirs may wish to retain the original.

Fight the good fight with all thy might · John Gardner (b. 1917)
When the Rev. James Monsell (1811-75) wrote and published these words in 1863, he could never have dreamed that they would be set to music a century later in such an infectiously rhythmical way. Rector of St. Nicolas Church, Guildford, at the time, he based the opening lines on St. Paul's first Epistle to Timothy (Ch. 6, v. 12) and it was sung to two tunes, *Duke Street* (still widely used today) and *Pentecost*.

John Gardner's music brings us right up to date with its catchy melody and strong rhythms and from the opening moments of the introduction (originally for piano), you can almost feel yourself marching into battle to 'fight the good fight'! Notice the metronome marking and the *Alla marcia* instruction. Obviously, rhythmic singing is the order of the day here, and some decisions will need to be made as to where to put the final consonants of such words as 'might', 'right', 'prize' etc. – my inclination would be to put the final consonant on the tied quaver rather than after it. One tip about learning this is to ask your choir to *say* the words in time, and when that is tidy, then is the time to move on to the notes. This is great fun to sing and just remember that singers need to 'look the part' as well as just getting the words and notes right.

For the beauty of the earth · John Joubert (b. 1927)
Born in Cape Town, John Joubert studied composition at the Royal Academy of Music, London, and went on to teach at the Universities of Hull and Birmingham. His hymn tune *Moseley* takes its title from the district of Birmingham in which he lives, and he has specially arranged it into anthem form for this book. Although written with a 6/8 time signature, choir conductors may find it easier to conduct the verses in four (12/8) and this may also help to avoid any unnecessary word stresses – e.g. 'of' and 'from' in verse 1. In the last verse it may be advisable to ask the second sopranos to sing the melody with the altos, thus giving it more weight than the descant.

The text dates from 1863 and the author, Folliot Sandford Pierpoint (1835-1917) originally intended it to be sung during the Communion – the refrain reading 'Christ our God, to thee we raise this our sacrifice of praise'. With the author's agreement, this was later altered to the present text, thus making the hymn more suitable for occasions of general thanksgiving.

Here I am, Lord · Daniel Schutte (b. 1947), arr. Malcolm Archer
Here is one of the most popular modern-style hymn-songs of recent years, with its memorable

tune, and text, based on Chapter 6 of Isaiah. Both the words and music are by Daniel Schutte, and were written in the 1970s whilst he was a student at the Jesuit Seminary in St. Louis, Missouri. Now living in San Francisco, he continues to write music for parish worship and is also in demand as a lecturer on liturgy.

Malcolm Archer's new arrangement was made for a recording by his choir at Wells Cathedral and immediately catches the rhythmic impulse of the music. The first two verses could be sung by soloists, and the simple yet effective block-chordal harmony of the refrain fits well against the running accompaniment. You will need to persuade your singers that the vocalised descant over the last chorus should not dominate the texture, but simply decorate it at a volume which will allow the melody and words of the tenors and basses to be audible. The quiet ending is very effective and, as elsewhere in the arrangement, the right hand could play the quavers (eighth notes) on a solo stop.

A Hymn for St. Cecilia · Herbert Howells (1892-1983)

Herbert Howells' music dates from 1959 and was written in response to a commission from the Livery Club of the Worshipful Company of Musicians of which he was the Master at that time. The poem, by Ursula Vaughan Williams, bears the title *A Hymn for St. Cecilia*, the patron saint adopted by musicians in the late fifteenth century, and since then honoured in paintings, poetry and musical composition, as well as the regular yearly celebrations at St. Ceciliatide (22nd November) including the Festal Evensong in St. Paul's Cathedral at which this anthem was first performed.

Written with the cathedral's generous acoustic in mind, the graceful arching phrases perfectly match the text, and make an immediate impact by using unison voices in the first verse. Here, as elsewhere, it would be helpful if either the choir director or one of the singers could read the poem aloud to the rest of the choir, for there are some awkward 'carry-overs' in places – e.g. 'and gather the clear sound into celestial joy' (verse 1). Be careful at the start of verse 2 that the text and melody of the tenors and basses is not obscured by the altos and sopranos, and the same applies to the descant in verse 3, though here, the altos join the tenors and basses in singing the melody. The composer did say that this descant 'should be sung whenever possible, but could be omitted if need be'. With an unfamiliar text such as this, diction is all important and for the sake of your listeners you may need to work harder than usual on such words as 'fountain's spray' and 'as sunlight'.

Jesus, fount of consolation · melody by Johann Freylinghausen (1670-1739), arr. Godfrey Sampson (1902-49)

This melody, and that of the following item, first appeared in the *Musicalisches Gesang-Buch*, containing 954 sacred songs and arias, old and new, for voice and figured bass, published by Georg Christian Schemelli in Leipzig in 1736. Attributed to Johann Freylinghausen, it was freely arranged into this anthem by Godfrey Sampson. The original title was *Jesus, unser Trost und Leben* (Jesus, our comfort and life) and the English text used here was written by Canon John Troutbeck (1832-99) of Westminster Abbey. The arranger has been assiduous in marking dynamics and if you observe them, your choir will not only convey the meaning of the text but also sing with a good deal of musical light and shade. Note the gradual crescendo to the climax of the verses at the repeated *Hallelujahs* and the strong unison passage at bars 45-48.

Jesus is the brightest light · melody by Johann Freylinghausen (1670-1739), inner parts, Gavin Williams (b. 1942)

This second melody from the Schemelli collection (see *Jesus, fount of consolation*) sets the text *Jesus ist das schönste Licht* by Christian Friedrich Richter (1676-1711). Since the late 19th century it has been available in an SATB version both in German and English and here, this realisation of the mean (middle) parts is by Gavin Williams, formerly sub-organist of Guildford Cathedral and now Director of Music at the King's School, Rochester, Kent.

It is a beautifully luminous melody and the flowing parts for ATB help to give the phrases a sense of movement. Ideally it should be sung unaccompanied, but it is also possible to have a light accompaniment, perhaps not doubling the melody – more like a continuo part.

Let all mortal flesh keep silence · 17th century French carol, arr. Rogers Covey-Crump (b. 1944)

The origins of the words are from the fourth century Liturgy of St. James, originally translated in 1868 and then versified by the Rev. Gerard Moultrie (1829-85), chaplain of Shrewsbury School. The now popular melody first appeared in the *English Hymnal* of 1906 and is described as a French carol from the 17th century. It is unusual in that it does not seem to have the dance-like feel often associated with carol melodies, but nevertheless it does seem to be a perfect match for the words.

The well known tenor Rogers Covey-Crump made this arrangement whilst he was a student at the Royal College of Music, where he was a first-study organist. The acoustics in your building may determine whether or not the humming ATB part in the first verse should break with the sopranos' punctuation, or if there should be a continuous humming throughout that verse. In verse 3, there needs to be very accurate tuning in the alto part, with those F sharps and naturals (and G naturals and G sharps) in the same bars, and it might be worth rehearsing the alto and tenor parts together before adding the bass and the top-line melody. For the last verse, the arranger has allowed himself some freedom from the confines of the melody, though you can spot fragments of it in this now major key, and the sopranos will need to be careful to observe the G sharps in bar 55 and not sing the version they sang in previous verses.

I'm sure your choir will enjoy singing this fresh-look version of such a familiar hymn.

Let all the world in ev'ry corner sing · George Dyson (1883-1964)

Following his training at the Royal College of Music, George Dyson became a public school music teacher and it was for his own choir that he wrote the original unison version of *Let all the world in ev'ry corner sing* as part of a collection entitled *Three Songs of Praise*. Some years later, the composer arranged it for SATB choir and also scored the accompaniment for string orchestra with optional brass and timpani.

George Herbert's poem is well known through its congregational use as well as in several other anthem settings and Dyson's music sets the text in a characteristic and grand way. Some performers (and listeners) may be startled by the sudden key change in bar 21, and it is here that the accompanist could use a touch of rubato, to savour that moment. Because of the loud volume of some of the high organ interludes (e.g. bars 7 and 20) your choir may have to overplay slightly their diction of the ends of such words as 'sing' and 'King'; otherwise these soft endings will not be audible or, worse still, may sound like 'sin' and 'kin'! At bars 9 to 10, it is possible for the sopranos to join the altos, and the tenors and sopranos should be prepared for the half-speed entry at bar 31, where they will also have to give a very firm vocal lead.

O perfect love · Joseph Barnby (1838-96)

The words were written in 1884 by Dorothy Frances Blomfield (1858-1932) for the wedding of her sister, and were originally intended to be sung to the tune 'Strength and Stay' by the Rev. J.B. Dykes (1828-76). Since then it has been linked to other tunes in various hymnals,

including the one by Joseph Barnby, which began life in its original anthem-form, as printed here. It was specially written for the wedding of the Duke and Duchess of Fife in 1889 while the composer was Precentor (Director of Music) at Eton College.

I've always thought that this is one of those melodies which sings itself, but it needs a tenderness in approach and an elegant sense of phrasing throughout. At the *più animato* section (bar 21 onwards) there should be more excitement in the sound of your choir, and likewise in the build-up around bars 60 to 62. As the composer states, the whole anthem may be sung with or without accompaniment. One small vocal tip, for this is one of those hymns which has the same mouth movements on two different letters of the alphabet: F (Life) and V (Love), one of which is sung (the V) and one of which is said (the F). You will need to work carefully with these, otherwise the listener could end up hearing Life and Luff !

Rejoice, the Lord is King! · Bryan Kelly (b. 1934)

An exciting and effervescent setting of a text usually sung by congregations to the strong but rather square tune by Handel. The text is by Charles Wesley (1707-88) with its refrain based on Philippians 4, verse 4 ('Rejoice in the Lord always: again I say, rejoice'), and originally there were 6 verses; most hymnals now use the four which are set here.

Bryan Kelly studied composition at the Royal College of Music and later returned there to teach. His setting of the Evening Canticles based on Latin-American rhythms (published by Novello in 1965) remains a favourite with many church and cathedral choirs. This setting of *Rejoice, the Lord is King!* was written in 1969 and its rhythmic verve brings new life to the text. In order to maintain the rhythm, it will be necessary to shorten the notes at the ends of certain words – 'rejoice', 'king', 'thanks', 'sing' etc., and these endings will need some careful work if the choir is to sing them together. Also, please take care to observe the composer's markings to help the correct word stressing – these are clearly indicated.

There is a green hill far away · William Horsley (1774-1858), arr. Barry Rose (b. 1934)

This famous text was written in 1848 by Cecil Frances Humphreys (1818-95, later known by her married name of Mrs. C.F. Alexander) for a volume called *Hymns for Little Children*, especially to illustrate the words from the Apostles' Creed 'Suffered under Pontius Pilate, was crucified, dead, and buried'. At that time the author was living not far from Londonderry in Northern Ireland, and the imagery of the 'green hill' and the 'city wall' (verse 1) most probably came from her visits there – she later changed the word 'without' to 'outside'. William Horsley's now familiar melody had been published four years earlier, in a collection entitled *Twenty-four Psalm Tunes* and Miss Humphreys may well have had this in mind when she wrote her poem.

The arrangement published here was made in March 1991, for the Chapel choir of Bramdean School, Exeter to sing in a broadcast of Choral Evensong. The two soprano parts in verses 3 and 4 are interchangeable and care should be taken at these points to see that the tune is always slightly louder than the other parts.

There's a wideness in God's mercy · Maurice Bevan (b. 1921)

The distinguished baritone Maurice Bevan wrote the original tune to these words in 1990, to be sung in St. Paul's Cathedral, in whose choir he had been a Vicar-Choral for 40 years. He called it 'Corvedale', after an area in Shropshire, around the River Corve, and near the village of Stanton Lacey where his father had been vicar. It was later extended into the anthem version published here. The text is from a longer poem of thirteen verses by Frederick William Faber (1814-63) who, as a convert to the Roman Catholic Church, came under the influence of Cardinal John Henry Newman and was one of the founders of London's Brompton Oratory.

You can almost feel the 'wideness in God's mercy' through Maurice Bevan's grand and spacious melody. I would suggest that this is one of those less familiar texts which you might ask your choir to read through (silently, or aloud) *before* they start learning the music.

This joyful Eastertide · 17th century Dutch carol, arr. William H. Harris (1883-1973)

The text of this much loved Eastertide carol dates from the early twentieth century, when it was written by the Rev. G.R. Woodward (1848-1934). He then matched it to its now well known tune, in the first edition of *The Cowley Carol Book*, of which he was the literary and musical editor. Since then it has been sung countless times in that version, with Charles Wood's harmony, and in 1958, Novello published this extended anthem-style arrangement by William Harris, then organist at St. George's Chapel, Windsor. As the arranger suggests, it needs a certain lightness in the singing of the unaccompanied sections, and getting the right speed is also most important – note the time

signature, which points us towards two beats in a bar, rather than four. Please take care to observe the printed dynamics and especially the build-up from a soft start to the last verse (bar 61) up to the final climax of the repeated 'arisen' (bar 85 onwards).

When I needed a neighbour, were you there? · Sydney Carter (b. 1915), arr. Barry Rose (b. 1934)

A favourite with the younger generation, *When I needed a neighbour* is now to be found in many hymn books. Both the words and the music are by the songwriter, poet and folk-singer Sydney Carter, also well-known for his *One more step along the world I go* and *Lord of the Dance*. Its message of social conscience, alluding to the parable of the Good Samaritan, is matched to a catchy melody set in a minor key, and this arrangement was made for the BBC Singers to sing on the Radio 4 Daily Service.

The real challenge in performance is to keep the volume in the choir very soft, both at the rhythmic opening and whilst they are accompanying the soloists. In contrast, verse 3 should be sung firmly and passionately, as should the final verse. Tenors will need to take care that they are ready to pick up the harmony again in bar 28 after their unison verse. In small choirs, it is quite possible to have the melody of the last verse sung by the two soloists, whilst the choir sings the 'descant' part.

Blessed are the pure in heart

John Keble

Henry Walford Davies

Lord is theirs,— Their soul is Christ's a - bode.—

Still to the low - ly soul He doth Him-self im - part,— And

for His cra - dle— and His throne,— Chóos - eth the pure in heart.—
[dwel - ling]

Brightest and best *

Bishop Reginald Heber

Eric Thiman

*from the Cantata *The Nativity*

© Copyright 1934 Novello & Company Limited

Star of the east, the ho - ri - zon a - dorn - ing, dorn - ing, dorn - ing,

Guide where our in - fant Re - deem - er is laid.

Sw. *p dolce*

(Man.)

SOPRANO

Cold on his cra - dle the dew - drops are shin - ing;

Low lies his head with the beasts of the stall;

An - gels a - dore him in slum - ber re - clin - ing,

Ma - ker and Mon - arch and Sa - viour of all.

QUARTET or SEMICHORUS

Say, shall we yield him, in__ cost-ly__ de-

-vo - tion,__ O - dours of E - dom, and__ of - f'rings di - vine,

SEMI-CHORUS or FULL

Gems of the moun - tain,__ and__ pearls of the o - cean,

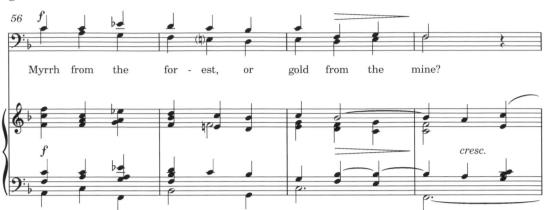

Myrrh from the for - est, or gold from the mine?

poco rall.

poco meno mosso

FULL

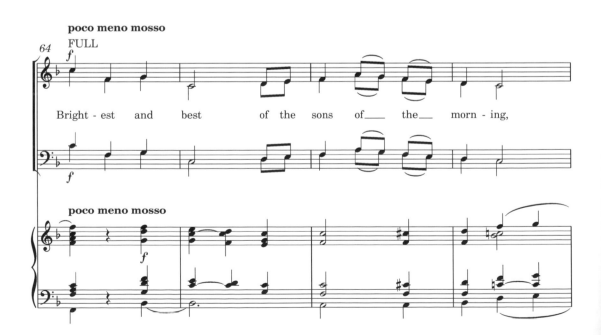

Bright - est and best of the sons of___ the___ morn - ing,

poco meno mosso

Dawn on our dark - ness, and lend us thine aid;

Star of the east, the__ ho - ri - zon a - dorn - ing, dorn - ing, ing,

dorn - ing,

Guide where our in - fant Re - deem - er__ is laid.

rall.

a tempo, meno mosso

mp Gt. Fl.

p Sw.

Ch. Clar.

molto rall.

poco marcato

for Malcolm Williamson

Fight the good fight with all thy might

Rev. J. S. B. Monsell

John Gardner
Op. 54, No. 5

By John Gardner from *Five Hymns in Popular Style*
© Copyright 1964 Oxford University Press. Reproduced by permission.

God's good grace, Lift up thine eyes_ and seek his face; Life with its way be -

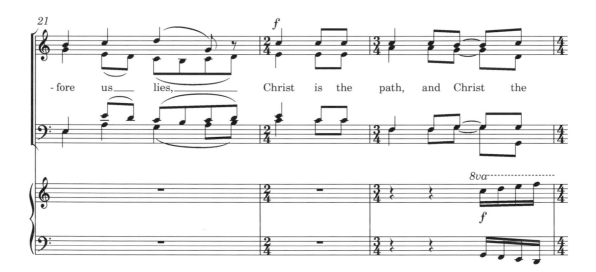

- fore us_ lies,_ Christ is the path, and Christ the

prize.___

3. Cast care a-side, lean

(T.)

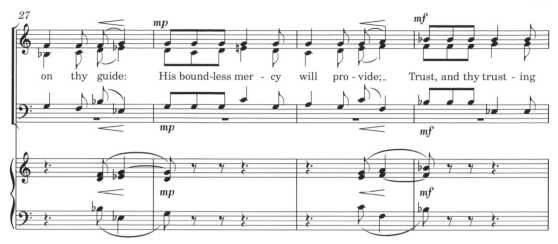

on thy guide: His bound-less mer - cy will pro - vide;_ Trust, and thy trust - ing

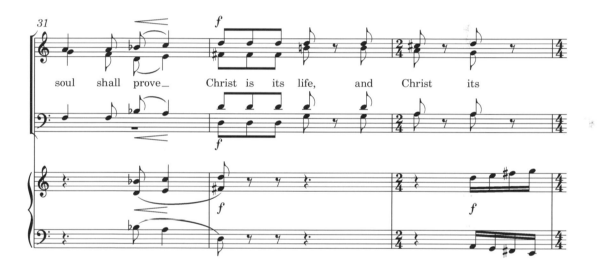

soul shall prove_ Christ is its life, and Christ its

love.__ 4. Faint not, nor fear, his

arms are near;___ He chang - eth not, and thou art

dear;___ On - ly be - lieve, and thou shalt see That

Christ is all in all to

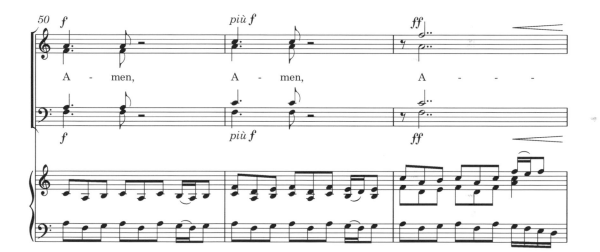

For the beauty of the earth

Hymn-anthem on the tune 'Moseley'

F.S. Pierpoint

John Joubert

This_ our grate-ful hymn_ of praise.

S.
A.

2. For___ the beau - ty of___ each hour_____ Of___ the day___ and
4. For___ each per - fect gift___ of thine_____ To___ our race___ so

T.
B.

of___ the night,___ Hill__ and vale__ and tree__ and flow'r,___
free - ly giv'n,___ Gra - ces hu - man and__ di - vine,___

Sun_ and moon and stars of light:_ Lord_ of all,_ to thee_ we raise_
Flowr's of earth and buds_ of heav'n:_

This_ our grate-ful hymn_ of praise._

5. For thy church which e-ver-more_ Lift-eth ho-ly

5 August 2000

Here I am, Lord

Words based on Isaiah, Ch. 6

Daniel Schutte, S. J.
arr. Malcolm Archer

V.1 SOPRANOS *mf* I, the Lord of sea and sky, I have heard my
V.2 TENORS AND BASSES *mp* I, the Lord of snow and rain, I have borne my
V.3 FULL *f* I, the Lord of wind and flame, I will tend the

peo - ple cry. All who dwell in dark and sin My hand will
peo - ple's pain. I have wept for love of them. They turn a -
poor and lame. I will set a feast for them. My hand will

Is it I, Lord?_____ I have heard You

call - ing in the night._____ I will go, Lord,_____

hold Your

if You lead me._____ I will hold__ Your__

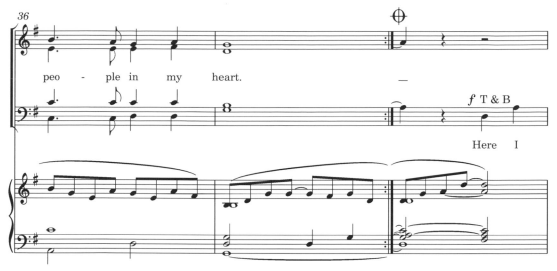

peo - ple in my heart.

ƒ T & B

Here I

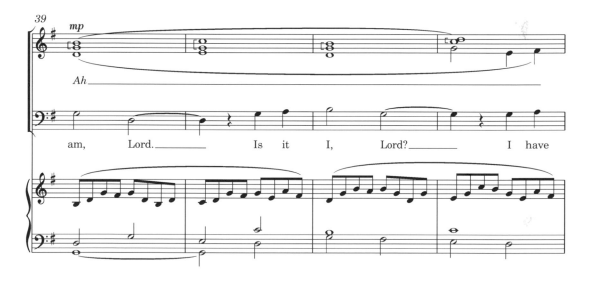

Ah

am, Lord. Is it I, Lord? I have

Ah

heard You call - ing in the night. I will

A Hymn for St. Cecilia

Ursula Vaughan Williams

Herbert Howells

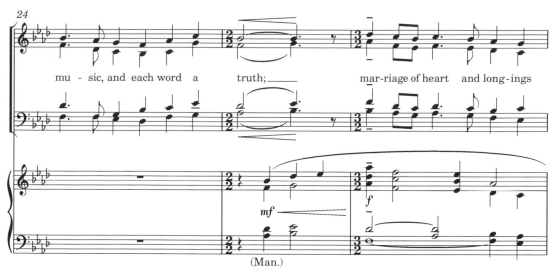

mu - sic, and each word a truth;_____ mar-riage of heart and long-ings

(Man.)

that as - pire, a bond of ro - ses, and a ring of fire._____

Ped.

Your sum - mer-time grows short and fades a - way, ter - ror must ga - ther to a

-ces in the skies, _____ Ce-ci-lia's

cen-tu-ries Ce-ci-lia's mu-sic dan-ces in the skies,

mu - sic _____ dan - - -

lend us a frag-ment of the im-mor-tal air, that with your

- - - ces in___ the skies.

choir-ing an-gels we may share, a word to

from _____ the earth a song _____
light us thro' time-fet-tered night, wa-ter of life, or rose of

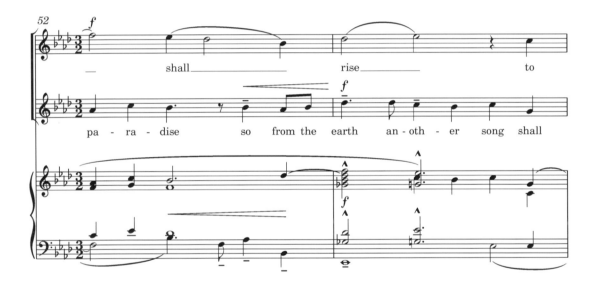

_ shall _____ rise _____ to
pa - ra - dise so from the earth an-oth - er song shall

meet _____ in heav'n's _____ de - light.
rise _____ to meet your own in heav'n's long _____ de - light.

Jesus, fount of consolation

English words by Rev. John Troutbeck

Melody by Johann Freylinghausen
arr. Godfrey Sampson

11

cresc.
Who___ through heav'n - ly love___ and might,

p cresc.
Who___ through heav'n - ly love and might,

cresc.
Who___ through love and might,___

p cresc.
Who___ through heav'n - ly love___ and might,

cresc.

15

f
Death - less life___ has brought to___ light,

f
Death - less life___ has brought to light,

f
Death - less life___ has brought to light,

f
Death - less life___ has brought to light,

f

He is held of death no long-er,
He is held of death no long-er,
Man.

He than death it-self is strong-er.
cresc.
Ped.

Fierce - ly though_ they rage and_ roar.

Fierce - ly though_ they rage and_ roar.

Fierce - ly though_ they rage and_ roar.

Fierce - ly though_ they rage and_ roar.

Zi - on right-ly_____ then re - joi - ces:

Zi - on right - ly then_ re - joi - ces:

Zi - on right-ly_____ then re - joi - ces:

Zi - on right - ly then_ re - joi - ces:

Man.

Jesus is the brightest light

Original German by C. F. Richter

Melody by Johann Freylinghausen
Inner parts by Gavin Williams

Je - sus___ is___ the___ fair - est___ name,
Lay___ but___ Je - sus___ to___ thine___ heart,

E'er___ by___ man___ or___ An - gel___ spo - ken,
Chas - ing___ far___ des - pair___ and___ sad - ness,

Sav - ing___ health_ it___ doth___ be - to - ken,
Name,_ in___ heav'n_ and___ earth,_ of___ glad - ness:

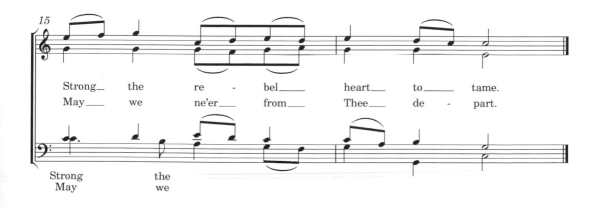

Strong___ the re - bel___ heart___ to___ tame.
May___ we ne'er___ from___ Thee___ de - part.

Strong the
May we

Let all mortal flesh keep silence

Liturgy of St. James
tr. Gerard Moultrie

17th century French carol
arr. Rogers Covey-Crump

44

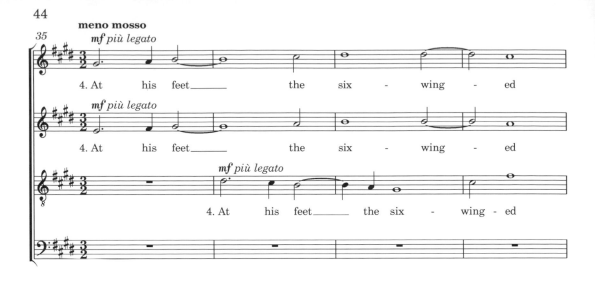

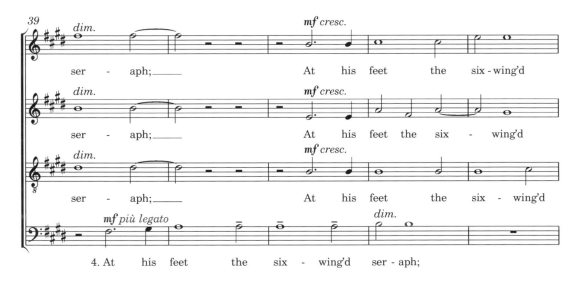

Let all the world in ev'ry corner sing

George Herbert

George Dyson

Originally entitled *Praise*, no. 1 of *Three Songs of Praise*

O perfect love

Wedding anthem

Dorothy Frances Blomfield

Joseph Barnby

glo-rious un-known mor - row, That dawns__ up - on e - ter - nal love and

glo-rious un-known mor - row, That dawns__ up - on e - ter - nal love and

glo-rious un-known mor - row, That dawns up - on e - ter - nal love and

glo - rious mor - row, That dawns up - on e - ter - nal love and

life,_____ And to life's day the glo - rious_____

life,_____ And to life's day_____ and to life's day the glo - rious

life, And to life's day, and to life's day the glo - rious

life,_____ And to life's day the glo - rious

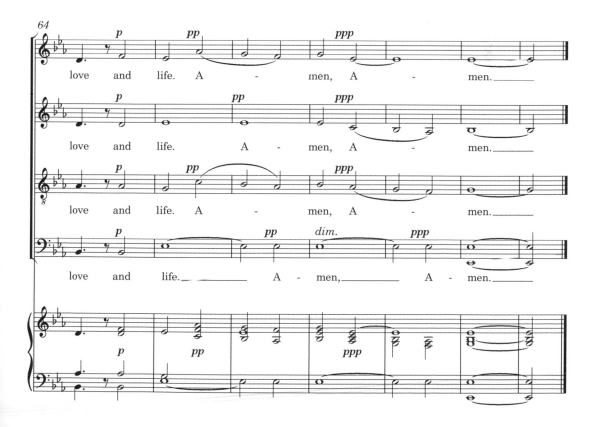

Rejoice, the Lord is King!

Charles Wesley

Bryan Kelly

thanks, give thanks and sing, And tri - umph e - ver - more:

Lift up your heart, lift up your voice; Re - joice, a -

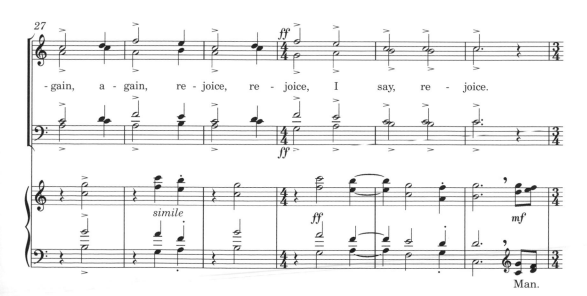

-gain, a - gain, re - joice, re - joice, I say, re - joice.

* voices alone ad lib.

- sus, Je - sus, the_ Sav - iour, reigns, The_ God_ of

truth_ and love; When he had purged our stains, He took_ his

seat, he took his seat a - bove: Lift up your

Re - joice, a - gain, a -

Re - joice,____ a - gain,____

- gain, re - joice, re - joice, I say, re - joice.

___ I say, re - joice,____ a - gain,___ re - joice.

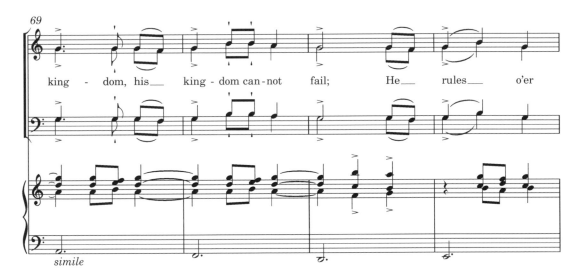

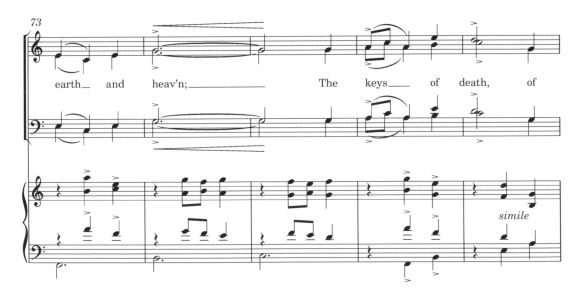

There is a green hill far away

Mrs C. F. Alexander

William Horsley
arr. Barry Rose

on - ly could un - lock the gate of heaven, and let us in.

on - ly could un - lock the gate of heaven, and let us in.

on - ly could un - lock the gate of heaven, and let us in.

on - ly could un - lock the gate of heaven, and let us in.

Ped.

mf

Allargando   DESCANT
mf

O

ALL OTHER VOICES
f

O

(add)   (add)   **Allargando**

gradual swell

solo reed

dear - ly has he loved, And we must love him too,_____ And

dear - ly, dear - ly has he loved, And we must love him too,_____ And

trust in his re - deem - ing blood, And try his works to do.

trust in his re - deem - ing blood, And try his works to do.

There's a wideness in God's mercy

F. W. Faber

Maurice Bevan

By Maurice Bevan, originally published in *Love Divine: Four Extended Hymns*
(Church Music Society Publication O26).
© Copyright 1999 Oxford University Press

-ty. There is no place where earth's sor - rows Are more

felt than up in heav'n; There is no place where earth's fail - ings Have such

kind-ly judge - ment giv'n.

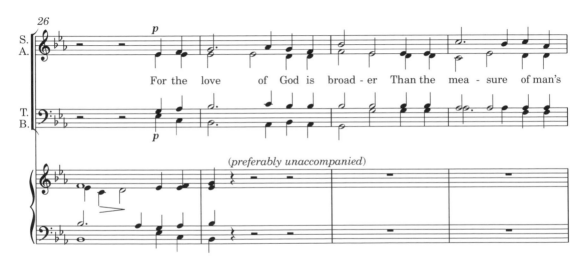

For the love of God is broad - er Than the mea - sure of man's

(*preferably unaccompanied*)

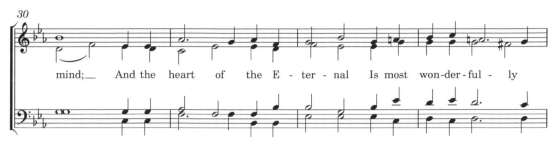

mind;__ And the heart of the E - ter - nal Is most won-der-ful - ly

kind. But we make his love too nar - row By false li - mits of our

own;____ And we mag - ni - fy his strict - ness With a

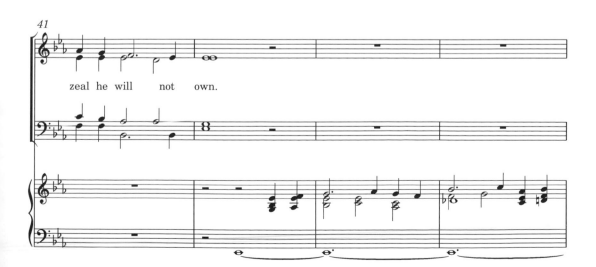

zeal he will not own.

poco rit.   **a tempo**

FULL UNISON

There is plen - ti - ful re - demp - tion In the blood that has been

shed; There is joy for all the mem-bers In the sor-rows of the

Head. There is grace e - nough for thou-sands Of new worlds as great as

This joyful Eastertide

Rev. G. R. Woodward

17th century Dutch carol
arr. William H. Harris

The unaccompanied sections may be lightly accompanied.
*The words are taken from *The Cowley Carol Book*, by permission of A. R. Mowbray & Co. Ltd.

Christ, that once was_ slain, Ne'er burst His three - day pri - son, Our

p

p

faith had been in vain: But now hath Christ a - ris - en,_ a - ris - en,_ a -

mf *cresc.*

mf *cresc.*

- ris - en, a - ris - - - - en.

f

f

f

SOPRANOS *mf*

My flesh in hope shall rest, And for a sea-son

(Sw.)

mf

(Gt.)

Man.

36

S. slum - - ber:

T.
B. Till trump from east to west Shall

Ped.

40

S.
A. Had Christ, that once was

T.
B. wake the dead in num - - ber.

44

slain, Ne'er burst His three-day pri - son, Our faith had been in vain: But

now hath Christ a - ris - en,_ a - ris - en,_ a - ris - en, a -

- ris - - - - en.

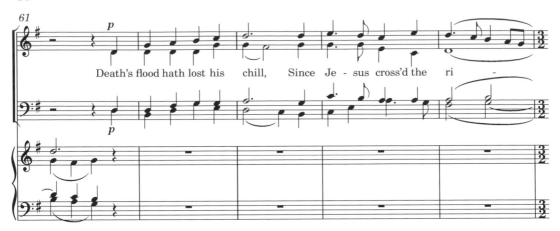

Death's flood hath lost his chill, Since Je - sus cross'd the ri -

from ill My
- ver: Lóv - er of souls, from ill___ My___ pass - ing soul de -
from ill___
Man.

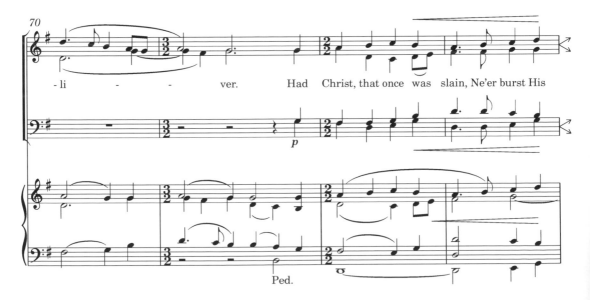

-li - - - ver. Had Christ, that once was slain, Ne'er burst His

Ped.

When I needed a neighbour, were you there?

Words and music by Sydney Carter
arr. Barry Rose

creed and the col-our and the name won't mat-ter, were you there?

_Ah_ _____

_Ah_ _____

ORGAN

_mp_

ALTO SOLO

_mp_

2. I was hun - gry and thir - sty, were you

_p_

_Mm_ _____

_p_

there, were you there? I was hun - gry and thir-sty, were you there? And the

_Oo_ _____

_Oo_ _____

_Oo_ _____ The

_mm_ _____

_Oo_ _____

creed and the col-our and the name won't mat-ter, were you there?

creed, col-our, name matter there?

name won't mat - ter there?

(+ soft Reeds)

mf cresc.

(Ped.)

TENORS & BASSES
mf passionately

3. I was cold, I was na-ked, were you there, were you there? I was

cold, I was na-ked, were you there? And the

creed and the col-our and the name won't mat-ter, were you there?

ALTO SOLO

4. When I need - ed a shel - ter, were you there, were you there? When I need - ed a shel - ter, were you

ALTO & BARITONE or TENOR SOLO

there? And the creed and the col-our and the name won't mat-ter, were you

The creed, col-our, name won't mat - ter

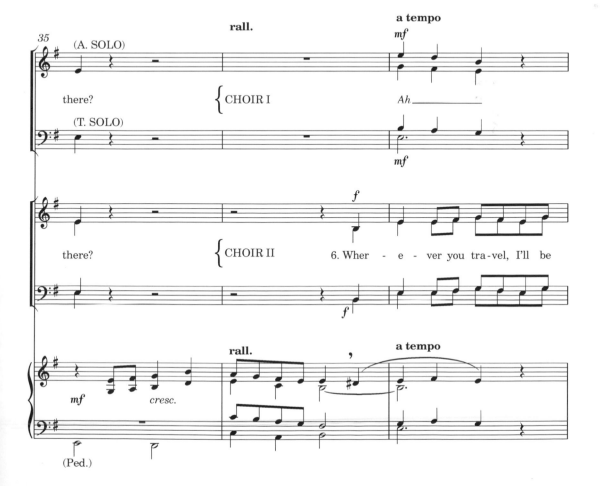

(A. SOLO)

there?

CHOIR I

Ah

(T. SOLO)

there?

CHOIR II

6. Wher - e - ver you tra-vel, I'll be

(Ped.)